Saint Peregrine
with Prayers and Devotions

Edited by
Mark Etling

Nihil Obstat: Reverend Robert O. Morrissey, J.C.D.
Censor librorum
March 24, 2003

Imprimatur: Most Reverend William Murphy
Bishop of Rockville Centre
March 31, 2003

THE REGINA PRESS
10 Hub Drive
Melville, New York 11747

All rights reserved. No part of this publication may be reproduced or transmitted in any form or by any means, electronic or mechanical, including photocopying, recording, or any information storage and retrieval system, without permission in writing from the publishers.

© Copyright 2003 by The Regina Press
Artwork © Copyright 2003 by Reproducta, NY.
Book design and typography by The Regina Press.

Florentine Collection™, All rights reserved worldwide.
Imported exclusively by Malco.

Printed in U.S.A.

ISBN: 0-88271-747-2

Introduction

One of the most important, yet most difficult, aspects of the spiritual life is maintaining trust in the will of God. Throughout our lives our faith is tested by hardships and setbacks of all kinds – failure, sadness, illness and death.

St. Peregrine stands as a wonderful example of what it means to trust completely in God. For years he suffered with a horrible, painful cancer in his foot and leg and was about to lose the leg to amputation. Yet his faith never wavered, and his trust became a moment for God to manifest his awesome, mysterious power over sickness and health, life and death.

Cancer is a terrible disease, cruelly snatching life away from men and women, young and old, rich and poor alike. It causes great suffering and anxiety to both its victims and their families.

Everyone can name a family member or loved one who has been touched by cancer. We hope and pray for cancer patients to be healed, yet we know there are never any guarantees that our prayers will be answered. Cancer is one of those experiences in life that challenge our trust in God.

We can never be sure that we will receive what we ask from God – we pray and live in faith. But Christians are called to hope – hope that God is with us at every moment, both in life and death, both now and into eternity. St. Peregrine is surely a shining example of that hope, that confidence, that complete trust in God.

The Life of St. Peregrine

*H*ow many people can say their lives were changed dramatically, irrevocably, by just one experience? Probably very few. Yet just one event changed the life of St. Peregrine forever. And the deep faith that life-changing experience produced in him would lead to a dramatic manifestation of the mysterious, loving power of God.

He was born Peregrine Laziosi in the town of Forli, Italy, in 1265, the only son of affluent parents of the nobility. He lived a comfortable life as a youth, and became part of a group that opposed the pope.

In 1283, St. Philip Benizi, prior general of the Friar Servants of Mary (the Servites), came to Forli on behalf of Pope Martin IV to try to lead the people of Forli back to full communion with the Church. At the time Forli was under interdict, meaning that its people were excluded from participation in the Mass and sacraments.

St. Philip was driven out of the city with abusive language, rocks and clubs. During the altercation, Peregrine struck him on the face with his fist, knocking him down. Remarkably, St. Philip reacted as Christ commanded in the Gospel, offering Peregrine his other cheek. This deeply moved the young man, so much so that with tears he confessed his guilt and promised to change his life. Philip both consoled Peregrine and exhorted him to change his ways.

From that moment on Peregrine's life changed forever. He began to perform many good works and to show great compassion for the downtrodden. Eventually he joined the Servites at Siena and was ordained a priest.

Peregrine later journeyed back to his hometown of Forli and started a Servite house there. He became well known for his preaching and holiness, and for his devotion to the sick and the poor.

As was common among Christians in those days, Peregrine performed many difficult penances. One of them was to sleep on the bare ground with a stone for a pillow, or leaning against a wall. Another was to stand whenever it was not necessary for him to sit. It was said that Peregrine once went for thirty years without sitting down.

As a result he developed varicose veins and then a painful and repulsive cancer of the foot and leg. By the time Peregrine reached age 60, the doctors were no longer able to help him. Finally the physician Paolo Salazio visited him in the priory and decided he would amputate Peregrine's cancerous leg as soon as possible.

The night before the surgery Peregrine spent much time in prayer before the cross in the priory chapter room. He asked God for healing, but he prayed as well to accept God's will for him. In his sleep he had a vision of the crucified Jesus coming down from the cross and touching his cancerous leg. When Peregrine woke up the sores were healed and his foot and leg were completely cured.

Peregrine would live another twenty years, and his reputation as a great preacher and confessor continued. He died in 1345, and his body was laid to rest in the Servite church in Forli.

Peregrine was beatified by Pope Paul V in 1609, and canonized by Pope St. Benedict XIII in 1726. His feast day is May 4.

St. Peregrine is well known as the patron saint of cancer patients. The common depiction of the saint shows him with a cross in one hand, and holding up his habit with the other to reveal the leg that was healed.

Prayers to St. Peregrine

Prayer to St. Peregrine

O great St. Peregrine, you have been called "The Mighty," and "The Wonder-Worker," because of the numerous miracles which you have obtained from God for those who have had recourse to you. For so many years you bore in your own flesh this cancerous disease that destroys the very fiber of our being, and you had recourse to the source of all grace when the power of human beings could do no more. You were favored with the vision of Jesus coming down from his cross to heal your affliction. Ask of God and Our Lady, the cure of the sick whom we entrust to you. *(Pause here and silently recall the names of the sick for whom you are praying.)* Aided in this way by your powerful intercession, we shall sing to God, now and for all eternity, a song of gratitude for his great goodness and mercy. Amen.

A Prayer to St. Peregrine for One Suffering from Cancer

*D*ear St. Peregrine, I need your help.
I feel so uncertain of my life right now.
This serious illness makes me long for a
 sign of God's love.
Help me to imitate your enduring faith
 when you faced the ugliness of cancer
 and surgery.
Allow me to trust the Lord the way you
 did in this moment of distress.

I want to be cured, but right now I ask
 God for the strength to bear this cross in
 my life.
I seek the power to proclaim God's
 presence in my life despite the
 hardship, anguish and
 fear I now experience.

O glorious St. Peregrine,
 be an inspiration to me and petitioner of
 those needed graces from our loving
 Father. Amen.

St. Peregrine Novena

O God, you gave St. Peregrine an angel for a companion, the Mother of God for his teacher, and Jesus for the Physician of his infirmity. Grant, we beg you, through his merits, that on earth we may love our holy angel, the Blessed Virgin, and our Savior, and in heaven bless them forever. Grant that we may receive the favor we now ask, through Christ our Lord. Amen.

Pray one Our Father, Hail Mary and Glory Be with the invocation: St. Peregrine, pray for us.

Prayer to St. Peregrine

*S*t. Peregrine, you have given us an example to follow; as a Christian, you were steadfast in love; as a Servite you were faithful in service; as a penitent you humbly acknowledged your sin; afflicted, you bore suffering with patience. Intercede for us, then, with our heavenly Father so that we, steadfast, humble, and patient, may receive from Christ Jesus the grace we ask. Amen.

Prayer to St. Peregrine

We implore your powerful aid, St. Peregrine, for all whose lives are unworthy of their Christian vocation. May they be converted, as you were, by the good example of those who are obedient to the call of Christ.

We invoke your special help, St. Peregrine, for all who are in religious life, that they may remain faithful to their vows, as you did, and ever steadfast in their commitment to Christ.

We seek your merciful aid, St. Peregrine, especially for those afflicted or threatened by cancer, by any ailment of the foot, or by any incurable disease. Please help us quickly to find a cure for cancer, and a remedy for all our infirmities of body, mind and soul.

Aided in this way by your powerful intercession, we shall sing to God, now and for all eternity, a song of gratitude for his great goodness and mercy. Amen.

Prayer to St. Peregrine

Dear Apostle of Emilia and member of the Order of Mary, you spread the Good News by your word and by your life witnessed to its truth. In union with Jesus crucified, you endured excruciating sufferings so patiently as to be healed miraculously of cancer in the leg. If it is agreeable to God, obtain relief and cure for *(mention name here)* and keep us all from the dread cancer of sin. Amen.

Prayer to St. Peregrine

O glorious wonder worker, St. Peregrine, you who answered the divine call with a ready spirit, forsaking all the comforts of a life of ease and all the empty honors of the world, to dedicate yourself to God in the Order of his most holy Mother; you who labored manfully for the salvation of souls, meriting the title Apostle of Emilia; you who in union with Jesus crucified, endured the most painful sufferings with such patience as to deserve to be miraculously healed from an incurable wound in your leg by him with a touch of his divine hand: obtain for us, we pray, the grace to answer every call from God; enkindle in our hearts a consuming zeal for the salvation of souls; deliver us from the infirmities that so often afflict our bodies; and obtain for us the grace of perfect resignation to the sufferings which may be sent to us; so may we, imitating your virtues and tenderly loving our crucified Lord and his sorrowful Mother, be enabled to merit glory everlasting in paradise. We ask this in the name of Jesus the Lord. Amen.

Prayer to St. Peregrine

Lord Jesus, through the intercession of St. Peregrine, touch and heal our brothers and sisters who are ill. Fill us with hope in trials so that, like St. Peregrine, we may walk with faith. Amen.

Prayer to St. Peregrine

St. Peregrine, whom Holy Mother Church has declared patron of those suffering from cancer, I confidently turn to you for help in my present sickness.

I beg your kind intercession. Ask God to relieve me of this sickness, if it be his holy will. Plead with the Blessed Virgin Mary, the Mother of Sorrows, whom you loved so tenderly and in union with whom you have suffered the pains of cancer, that she may help me with her powerful prayers and loving consolation.

But if it should be God's holy will that I bear this sickness, obtain for me courage and strength to accept these trials from the loving hand of God with patience and resignation, because he knows what is best for the salvation of my soul.

St. Peregrine, be my friend and patron. Help me to imitate you in accepting suffering, and to unite myself with Jesus crucified and the Mother of Sorrows, as you did. I offer my pains to God with all the love of my heart, for his glory and the salvation of souls. Amen.

Litany in Honor of St. Peregrine

Lord, have mercy on us.
Christ, have mercy on us.
Lord, have mercy on us.
Christ, hear us.
Christ, graciously hear us.
God, the Father of heaven,
  have mercy on us.
God the Son,
  Redeemer of the world,
    have mercy on us.
God the Holy Spirit,
  have mercy on us.
Holy Trinity,
  one God, have mercy on us.
Holy Mary,
  Mother of God, pray for us.
Mother of Sorrows,
  pray for us.
Health of the sick,
  pray for us.
Comforter of the afflicted,
  pray for us.
Help of Christians, pray for us.

St. Peregrine,
  pray for us.
St. Peregrine,
  converted by the prayers of St. Philip,
    pray for us.
St. Peregrine,
  afflicted with a cancerous growth,
    pray for us.
St. Peregrine,
  completely cured by the outstretched
  hand of Jesus crucified,
    pray for us.
St. Peregrine,
  who performed many miracles
  in your lifetime,
    pray for us.
St. Peregrine,
  who multiplied food and drink,
    pray for us.
St. Peregrine,
  who cured the sick by the power
  of the name of Jesus,
    pray for us.
St. Peregrine,
  who converted hardened sinners by

prayer and fasting,
> pray for us.

St. Peregrine,
who received every favor you asked of God,
> pray for us.

St. Peregrine,
most confident in prayer,
> pray for us.

St. Peregrine,
most austere in penance,
> pray for us.

St. Peregrine,
most patient in suffering,
> pray for us.

St. Peregrine,
most humble in the holy priesthood,
> pray for us.

St. Peregrine,
most zealous for souls,
> pray for us.

St. Peregrine,
most kind toward the afflicted,
> pray for us.

St. Peregrine,
  most devoted to the Passion of Jesus
  and the Sorrows of Mary,
    pray for us.
St. Peregrine,
  victim with Jesus and Mary for the
  salvation of souls,
    pray for us.
St. Peregrine,
  wonder-worker for the sick and diseased,
    pray for us.
St. Peregrine,
  hope of incurable cases,
    pray for us.
St. Peregrine,
  universal patron of those afflicted with
  cancer and running sores,
    pray for us.
St. Peregrine,
  beloved patron of Spain,
    pray for us.
St. Peregrine,
  glory of the Order of the Servants of Mary,
    pray for us.

Lamb of God,
> who takes away the sins of the world, spare us, O Lord.

Lamb of God,
> who takes away the sins of the world, graciously hear us, O Lord.

Lamb of God,
> who takes away the sins of the world, have mercy on us.

Pray for us, O glorious St. Peregrine.
> That we may be made worthy of the promises of Christ.

Let us pray. O God, graciously hear the prayers which we present to you in honor of St. Peregrine, your beloved servant and patron of cancer patients, so that we, who do not rely on our own merits, may receive help in our needs through the intercession of him whose life had been so pleasing to you. Through Christ, our Lord. Amen.

Prayer to the Mother of Sorrows

*M*y dearest Mother, Virgin Mother of God and Mother of Sorrows, behold me, your child, in prayer before you. I plead for a special favor through the intercession of your faithful servant, St. Peregrine, who was so devoted to you.

Sorrowful Mother, I beg you to present my petition to your divine Son. I know you want me to seek God's will in all things, as you always did. Therefore, with childlike trust I abandon myself to God's holy will concerning my request. If what I ask for should not be granted, pray that I may receive that which will be of greater benefit to my soul.

Dear Mother of Sorrows, I love you! I put all my confidence in you, because your prayers before God are most powerful. For the sake of Jesus who suffered for my soul as you also did, and through the intercession of St. Peregrine, hear and grant my prayer. Amen.

Prayer for Someone Afflicted with Cancer

*L*ord Jesus Christ, you have willed that St. Peregrine should be invoked by thousands of persons as the patron of those suffering with cancer, and have caused that through his intercession many cures should be wrought. I thank you for this tender compassion for suffering humanity, and for answering the prayers of this compassionate saint. I recommend to you the following person *(mention the person or persons you wish to pray for)*.

Be pleased to hear the prayers of St. Peregrine, as well as those of your Blessed Mother, the Health of the Sick, on behalf of the person whom I recommend to the love and mercy of your Sacred Heart. Give him (her) patience in bearing suffering, and resignation to your divine will. Give him (her) the consolation he (she) needs and especially a cure, if it be your holy will.

Novena Prayer in Honor of St. Peregrine

Opening Novena Prayer:

Blessed St. Peregrine, you knew in your own body the reality of pain. You knew, too, the place of suffering in the life of Jesus. In his wisdom, God saw fit to heal you of your illness. We now ask you to intercede for us that we may be healed of our infirmities to the glory and praise of God, our Father through his Son Jesus. Amen.

Day One

For Cancer Patients.

Lord, you were moved to pity at the words of the leper, "If you want to, you can heal me." Heal all our brothers and sisters who suffer from cancer, and cure us of all the wounds of our sinfulness. We offer this prayer through you and in union with the Holy Spirit to the glory of God, our Father. Amen.

Day Two

For Those Healed.

Lord, you praised the leper who returned to give you thanks. We praise and thank you, now, for the healing you have brought about in many of our sisters and brothers. Keep alive in them the sense of gratitude and sustain them with your love that they may praise and glorify you in union with the Spirit to the honor of the Father. Amen.

Day Three

For the Doctors.

Lord, you were moved to pity at the request of the blind man, "Lord, that I may see." Fill with the vision of faith all doctors. Let them see in their patients the image of your own suffering and feel in their own hearts your compassion that they may always reverence those for whom they care, knowing them to be children of your Father. To him we offer our prayers in union with you and the Holy Spirit. Amen.

Day Four

For the Researchers.

*F*ather, you alone hold the keys to life and death. Yet, in your divine love for us, you have gifted your people with wondrous skill and intelligence in overcoming disease. Direct with your wisdom our brothers and sisters who work in cancer research that they may be faithful in the service of your children and successful in their efforts to combat this disease. We pray to you in Jesus' name. Amen.

Day Five

For the Nurses and Aides.

*L*ord, when you walked this earth, you were always moved to pity at the sight of suffering. Now it is through others that your compassion is made known. We pray for all nurses and aides who serve their brothers and sisters afflicted with cancer. Strengthen them when they are weary and fill their hearts with your love that they may reflect your care to those for whom they work. May their dedicated lives praise and glorify your Father. Amen.

Day Six

For the Family.

Lord, you were moved to pity by the tears of the widow of Nain. Dry the tears and comfort the hearts of those who are sad because their loved ones suffer. Support them when their courage falters and sustain them in patience that they in turn may be a source of peace to the suffering. Fill us all with a share in your tender compassion for the glory of God the Father. Amen.

Day Seven

For the Anxious.

Lord, you brought comfort and peace to the hearts of your friends when you spoke to them the words, "Fear not." Hear our prayers for all your children who are held captive by anxiety, especially those whose fear of cancer robs them of peace. Flood their hearts with trust in you that they may live in the freedom of the children of God. We pray with you to the glory of his name. Amen.

Day Eight
For the Terminally Ill.

Lord of life, the night before you died, you asked your Father to remove from you the cup of suffering if he so willed. Instead, he gave you the courage to accept death. Give courage, we beg you, to our brothers and sisters who suffer from terminal cancer. Lead them to serenity as they await the moment of unsurpassed joy, when they will see you, Love itself, face to face. We pray to the Father in union with you and the Holy Spirit. Amen.

Day Nine
For Healing.

Father, your Son accepted our sufferings in life and death. Hear our prayers for all our sick brothers and sisters. May all who suffer pain know that they are joined to Christ in his suffering for the salvation of the world, with you and the Holy Spirit, one God, forever and ever. Amen.

Closing Prayer:

Glorious St. Peregrine, we rejoice in the victory of you, our brother, and we ask you to remember us before the throne of God. While on earth, you were able because of your own deep faith, to counsel and console those who suffered in pain and in fear. Continue to help us all so that, through your brotherly care, we may be delivered from misfortune and strengthened in faith. We make our prayer in Jesus' name. Amen.

Prayer to St. Peregrine

O God, in St. Peregrine you gave us an outstanding example of faith and patience. We humbly ask you that, by imitating him and by the help of his prayers, we may believe more fully in your healing help, bear the suffering of this life without wavering, and come with joy to the peace of heaven. We ask this through Jesus Christ, our Lord. Amen.

Prayer to St. Peregrine, Patron Saint of Cancer

St. Peregrine, we come to you confidently to implore your aid with God in our necessity. You were converted instantly from a worldly life by the good example of one holy person. You were cured instantaneously of cancer by God's grace and unceasing prayer. In your gracious kindness please ask the Lord to heal us also in body, mind and soul. May we then imitate you in doing his work with renewed vigor and strength. Amen.

Prayer to St. Peregrine

Lord Jesus, through the intercession of St. Peregrine, touch and heal our brothers and sisters who are ill. Fill us with hope in trials so that, like St. Peregrine, we may walk in faith. Amen.

Prayer to St. Peregrine

O most holy St. Peregrine, God gave you an angel for your companion, the Mother of God for your teacher, and Jesus as the Physician of your illness. Obtain for me through your prayers a greater love for my holy Angel, the Blessed Virgin and our Savior. Amen.

Prayer to St. Peregrine

Graciously hear the prayers which we present O God, to you in honor of St. Peregrine, your beloved servant and patron of those suffering from cancer, or any life-threatening disease. Grant that we may receive help in our needs through the intercession of him whose life was so pleasing to you. Hear us in the name of Christ, our Lord. Amen.

Cancer Is Limited...

It cannot cripple love,
It cannot shatter hope,
It cannot corrode faith,
It cannot eat away peace,
It cannot destroy confidence,
It cannot shut out memories,
It cannot silence courage,
It cannot invade the soul,
It cannot reduce eternal life,
It cannot quench the spirit,
It cannot lessen the power
   of the Resurrection.